My Mornings Reflecting On The Lord

A Devotion Journal For Women

Activinotes

Date:

Scripture for the day:

My meditative thoughts:

Date:

Scripture for the day:

My meditative thoughts:

Date:

Scripture for the day:

My meditative thoughts:

Date:

Scripture for the day:

My meditative thoughts:

Date:

Scripture for the day:

My meditative thoughts:

Date:

Scripture for the day:

My meditative thoughts:

Date:

Scripture for the day:

My meditative thoughts:

Date:

Scripture for the day:

My meditative thoughts:

Date:

Scripture for the day:

My meditative thoughts:

Date:

Scripture for the day:

My meditative thoughts:

Date:

Scripture for the day:

My meditative thoughts:

Date:

Scripture for the day:

My meditative thoughts:

Date:

Scripture for the day:

My meditative thoughts:

Date:

Scripture for the day:

My meditative thoughts:

Date:

Scripture for the day:

My meditative thoughts:

Date:

Scripture for the day:

My meditative thoughts:

Date:

Scripture for the day:

My meditative thoughts:

Date:

Scripture for the day:

My meditative thoughts:

Date:

Scripture for the day:

My meditative thoughts:

Date:

Scripture for the day:

My meditative thoughts:

Date:

Scripture for the day:

My meditative thoughts:

Date:

Scripture for the day:

My meditative thoughts:

Date:

Scripture for the day:

My meditative thoughts:

Date:

Scripture for the day:

My meditative thoughts:

Date:

Scripture for the day:

My meditative thoughts:

Date:

Scripture for the day:

My meditative thoughts:

Date:

Scripture for the day:

My meditative thoughts:

Date:

Scripture for the day:

My meditative thoughts:

Date:

Scripture for the day:

My meditative thoughts:

Date:

Scripture for the day:

My meditative thoughts:

Date:

Scripture for the day:

My meditative thoughts:

Date:

Scripture for the day:

My meditative thoughts:

Date:

Scripture for the day:

My meditative thoughts:

Date:

Scripture for the day:

My meditative thoughts:

Date:

Scripture for the day:

My meditative thoughts:

Date:

Scripture for the day:

My meditative thoughts:

Date:

Scripture for the day:

My meditative thoughts:

Date:

Scripture for the day:

My meditative thoughts:

Date:

Scripture for the day:

My meditative thoughts:

Date:

Scripture for the day:

My meditative thoughts:

Date:

Scripture for the day:

My meditative thoughts:

Date:

Scripture for the day:

My meditative thoughts:

Date:

Scripture for the day:

My meditative thoughts:

Date:

Scripture for the day:

My meditative thoughts:

Date:

Scripture for the day:

My meditative thoughts:

Date:

Scripture for the day:

My meditative thoughts:

Date:

Scripture for the day:

My meditative thoughts:

Date:

Scripture for the day:

My meditative thoughts:

Date:

Scripture for the day:

My meditative thoughts:

Date:

Scripture for the day:

My meditative thoughts:

Date:

Scripture for the day:

My meditative thoughts:

Date:

Scripture for the day:

My meditative thoughts:

Date:

Scripture for the day:

My meditative thoughts:

Date:

Scripture for the day:

My meditative thoughts:

Date:

Scripture for the day:

My meditative thoughts:

Date:

Scripture for the day:

My meditative thoughts:

Date:

Scripture for the day:

My meditative thoughts:

Date:

Scripture for the day:

My meditative thoughts:

Date:

Scripture for the day:

My meditative thoughts:

Date:

Scripture for the day:

My meditative thoughts:

Date:

Scripture for the day:

My meditative thoughts:

Date:

Scripture for the day:

My meditative thoughts:

Date:

Scripture for the day:

My meditative thoughts:

Date:

Scripture for the day:

My meditative thoughts:

Date:

Scripture for the day:

My meditative thoughts:

Date:

Scripture for the day:

My meditative thoughts:

Date:

Scripture for the day:

My meditative thoughts:

Date:

Scripture for the day:

My meditative thoughts:

Date:

Scripture for the day:

My meditative thoughts:

Date:

Scripture for the day:

My meditative thoughts:

Date:

Scripture for the day:

My meditative thoughts:

Date:

Scripture for the day:

My meditative thoughts:

Date:

Scripture for the day:

My meditative thoughts:

Date:

Scripture for the day:

My meditative thoughts:

Date:

Scripture for the day:

My meditative thoughts:

Date:

Scripture for the day:

My meditative thoughts:

Date:

Scripture for the day:

My meditative thoughts:

Date:

Scripture for the day:

My meditative thoughts:

Date:

Scripture for the day:

My meditative thoughts:

Date:

Scripture for the day:

My meditative thoughts:

Date:

Scripture for the day:

My meditative thoughts:

Date:

Scripture for the day:

My meditative thoughts:

Date:

Scripture for the day:

My meditative thoughts:

Date:

Scripture for the day:

My meditative thoughts:

Date:

Scripture for the day:

My meditative thoughts:

Date:

Scripture for the day:

My meditative thoughts:

Date:

Scripture for the day:

My meditative thoughts:

Date:

Scripture for the day:

My meditative thoughts:

Date:

Scripture for the day:

My meditative thoughts:

Date:

Scripture for the day:

My meditative thoughts:

Date:

Scripture for the day:

My meditative thoughts:

Date:

Scripture for the day:

My meditative thoughts:

Date:

Scripture for the day:

My meditative thoughts:

Date:

Scripture for the day:

My meditative thoughts:

Date:

Scripture for the day:

My meditative thoughts:

Date:

Scripture for the day:

My meditative thoughts:

Date:

Scripture for the day:

My meditative thoughts:

Date:

Scripture for the day:

My meditative thoughts:

www.ingramcontent.com/pod-product-compliance
Lightning Source LLC
Chambersburg PA
CBHW080738250626
47170CB00010B/2877
* 9 7 8 1 6 8 3 2 1 0 5 7 3 *